Introduction

In this wonderful book of **Ribbon Embroidery Alphabets** you will find the perfect embellishments for personalizing everything from clothing to bed linens.

The front and back covers of this book show just a few of the letters actually stitched from each of the alphabets. Of course, we have included transfers for all 26 letters of all nine beautiful alphabets. In addition, there are some clever winged insects (butterflies, dragonfly and ladybug) and two hummingbirds for you to use for your project, if you so desire.

The first section of this book includes all the basic information you'll need to know to get started with ribbon embroidery. We've included a discussion of the *Supplies* we used, *Special Techniques* for ribbon, *The Stitches* needed for our alphabets, and *Using Iron-On Transfers*.

The center of this book has all the alphabets and winged creatures printed as transfers. They are reversed, so when ironed onto your fabric they will read correctly.

The last section is the *Alphabet Stitching Guides*. These guides show just one of the letters of each alphabet—that letter is also on the front or back cover. By following the information in these guides and referring to the cover photograph, you will be able to stitch any of the letters in the alphabets.

Supplies

Ribbon

Ribbons used for embroidery are chosen for their special properties and are now manufactured by a number of different companies. They must drape nicely and be able to be pulled through fabric without damage to the ribbon or the fabric. Silk, silky polyester, and rayon ribbons can be used for embroidery.

On the Stitching Guides for the alphabets (pages 47-56), we have listed the colors used for the front and back cover embroideries. Refer to the Color Conversion Key, page 57, for suggestions when substituting different brands of ribbon. Color ranges vary greatly between companies, so you can really choose whatever colors you want based on what is readily available and your own personal preference.

In ribbon embroidery, 4mm is the most commonly used ribbon size, and most companies will have a wide range of 4mm colors. The 2mm and 7mm ribbons are also used, although the color range is more limited. Mixing ribbon widths adds to the textural contrast which is such a strong aspect of this embroidery

Six-strand embroidery floss is occasionally used with the ribbon to create narrow lines of embroidery, tack down a portion of a stitch, or to preserve a special shape.

Fabric

Many different fabrics can be used for ribbon embroidery. Basically you will want to choose a fabric with a sturdy weave which also allows a needle to pass through easily. Avoid sheer fabrics. This embroidery is heavier than floss embroidery so it requires a stable base; also, ribbon ends tend to show through sheer fabrics. If a thin fabric must be used, underline it with another piece of fabric or woven interfacing for stability and to create a more opaque surface.

Choose a fabric that will complement the stitching and not compete in color or texture with the embroidery. Look for materials in fabric departments and needlework shops, including many of the evenweave fabrics used for cross stitch.

Pick a fabric that is light enough for the transfer to show, and check that your fabric choice can withstand the wool or cotton iron setting that is needed for the transfer. If you prefer a dark fabric, see Other Methods to Transfer Designs, page 5.

Be sure to cut fabric with plenty of extra margins on all sides of the design. Overcast the outside edges to prevent fraying.

The back of ribbon embroidery is certainly not neat! If you are working on a readymade garment, you might wish to remove enough of the lining to do your stitching, then replace the lining to cover back of work. If there is no lining, consider backing the stitching area with a soft material.

Ribbons and Floss

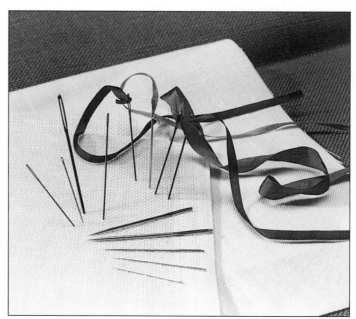

Needles and Fabrics

Needles and Scissors

Two different needle styles are recommended for ribbon embroidery. We find that both kinds have their place. You can choose a sharp chenille (or crewel) needle or a blunt tapestry needle. Be sure to choose long-eyed needles, and remember that the higher the number, the smaller the needle.

Chenille or crewel needles have long eyes and sharp points. Tightly woven fabrics will call for a sharp needle to pierce the fabric. A size 8 is a good all-purpose size, but we suggest an assortment pack with a 3-9 size range.

A tapestry needle will slide comfortably between the fabric threads and will not easily snag previous stitches. Tapestry needles make a nice hole in the fabric through which the ribbon can be pulled. Choose between sizes 20-26.

Choose some small, sharp-pointed good quality scissors for cutting ribbon. A clean angled cut will help prevent the cut edge from fraying. Store your scissors away from your embroidery to avoid harming ribbon or fabric.

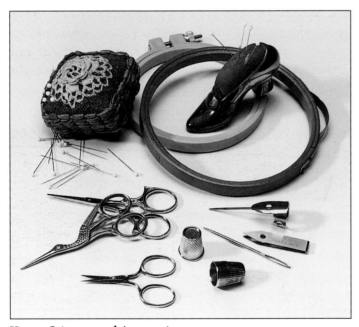

Hoops, Scissors, and Accessories

Hoops and Frames

For the best stitching results your fabric should be held taut while you stitch. Transfer your design before stretching it in a hoop or frame. A hoop works nicely only if the completed stitches will not be crushed by the hoop's rim. Never store an unfinished project in a hoop.

A scroll frame or stretcher bars that are large enough to contain the entire area of the design works very well. Make sure the design has already been transferred before attaching the fabric. A floor or table stand is also handy for keeping both hands free to manipulate the ribbon.

Stitching Tips

A wonderful advantage of working with ribbon is that the stitches can be made rather loosely, with moderate tension, or snugly. The same stitch may look different each time it is made—this is part of the charm of working with ribbon. Do be careful not to pull stitches so tightly that the ribbon looks like thread.

As you make each stitch, take care that the ribbon lies flat on the surface (unless you want it to twist). Also be sure when stitching down into the fabric that you do not pierce previously made stitches. A spare large tapestry needle can be used to coax the ribbon into position.

Follow the transfer lines and refer to the instructions for working your chosen alphabet (pages 47-56). Note that the transfer designs use symbols for each stitch which are slightly smaller than the actual stitches, so your embroidery will adequately cover the design lines. Make sure that the length or size of each stitch is just beyond its transfer line.

Don't carry your ribbon from one area to the next as you stitch. Not only will it possibly show through on the front, but as you stitch other colors in those areas, the carried ribbon will interfere.

Special Techniques

Threading the Needle

Always cut your ribbon into short lengths for stitching; we recommend 12"-14". Thread the end through the eye, and pull it through beyond the tip of the needle. Pierce the ribbon end with the needle, **Fig 1**. Holding point of needle, pull the long end of the ribbon to secure it.

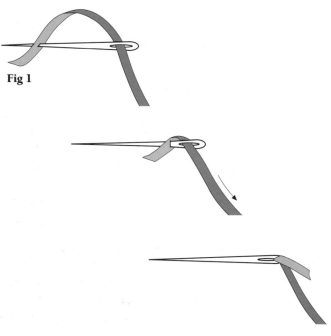

Fig 1

Making a Knot

To begin stitching, make this special knot, **Fig 2**, at the end of the ribbon. Drape ribbon end over needle; wrap working ribbon once around needle, then pull needle through the wrap to form a knot. When you begin to stitch, be careful not to pull too tightly, or the knot may come through the fabric.

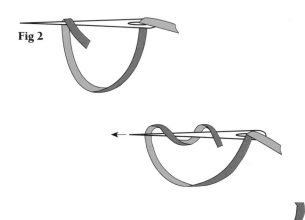

Fig 2

Ending the Ribbon

When you finish using a color, run the needle toward center of the stitching under a few stitches on the wrong side, **Fig 3**. This will keep ends from showing through on the right side. If desired, pierce through some ribbon on the back before cutting the end, making sure this does not disturb the front of your work.

wrong side of fabric

Blocking & Finishing

If your piece was worked on a frame, there will probably be no blocking required. If the finished embroidery is to be washed, pre-test the ribbon to make sure it is colorfast. Dip a small piece in water and place on a paper towel; let dry and check to see if the dye runs. If some embroidered ribbon becomes too limp, a slight spritz of water may refresh it.

When working on a readymade garment, take into account the surface fabric needs as well as the embroidery.

If you must take an iron to it, press face down on a thick padded surface—a terry cotton towel is an excellent choice—only lightly pressing the areas of stitching. Use caution to prevent scorching.

When framing, you may wish to protect the embroidery with glass. Because of the textural quality, choose a shadow box frame or insert spacers to keep the glass from touching the stitches.

Using Iron-On Transfers

Protect the ironing board surface with a piece of clean fabric or heavy brown wrapping paper. Before transferring, make a test run using a test pattern transfer (found on each transfer page) on a scrap of your fabric. Follow Steps 1 to 3 below for transferring. The results should be clear, but do not have to be dark (the transfers are designed to be used at least three times). If you are not satisfied, try again, adjusting the heat of the iron, the length of time or the amount of pressure you put on the iron. Different fabrics require heat adjustments as well as varying lengths of time. Also, no two irons heat the same way, so you must make this trial to ensure success. When you are satisfied with the test pattern trial, follow these steps for transferring designs.

> **Note:** *These are permanent iron-ons that will usually transfer three times. The lines will not wash out. Excess humidity may cause a transferred design to fade after it has been ironed onto the fabric. If humidity is high, do not transfer the designs until you are ready to use them.*

1. Preheat dry iron to between wool and cotton setting. Place fabric on ironing board, right side up, with transfer pinned ink side down. Center the transfer with the straight grain of the fabric running vertically and allowing plenty of room on each side for finishing, **Fig 4**. Keep pins to outside of design lines, in the margins if possible.

2. Cover design area with a paper towel or tissue paper. Place the hot iron on the paper towel and hold for 10 to 15 seconds (or the length you determine with your test pattern). Lift the iron straight up and down, applying an even pressure to all parts of the design. Do not move iron back and forth. Lift the iron and replace it several times so that areas under steam holes are transferred.

> **Hint:** *To get a better impression, especially on a second or third usage of a transfer, place a piece of aluminum foil under the fabric. You may also need to increase the pressing time.*

3. Carefully lift one corner of the transfer and check that the design has printed. Do not remove pins until you are completely satisfied with the transfer; it is almost impossible to realign once it has been moved. If you are not satisfied, repeat Step 2. When transferring is completed, unpin and peel off transfer; keep the design handy to refer to while stitching.

Other Methods to Transfer Design

If transfer ink doesn't show up on a dark fabric or you have used up the ink, the design can be easily transferred using a transfer pen or pencil or dressmaker's carbon, available at craft and fabric stores. Choose a light color for dark fabrics; and a dark color for light fabrics. Turn pattern inked side up and trace original design. Transfer following manufacturer's instructions.

Joan Messenger
30 Ridgewood Rd
Sunapee NH 03782-3124

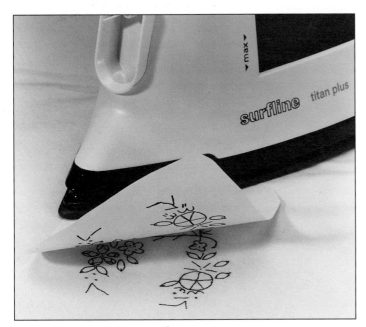

Fig 4 - Using Iron-On Transfers

The Stitches

Some basic embroidery stitches are known by different names, but we have chosen the most commonly used titles. Unless otherwise directed, bring ribbon up from back to front of fabric at odd (1, 3, 5) numbers and stitch down through fabric at even (2, 4, 6) numbers. The stitches required, ribbon colors used, and special notes are given for each of the nine alphabets beginning on page 47. When floss is required, use two strands unless otherwise directed.

The designs use symbols to show the shape of each stitch in addition to the placement. Following is a list of the symbols and the stitches they represent.

Symbols for Stitches

+++ = Couching

• = French Knot

𝒪 = Lazy Daisy Stitch

0 = Loop Stitch

" = Padded Straight Stitch

'. = Pistil Stitch

𝒪 = Ribbon Stitch

𝒪 = Side Ribbon Stitch

⊕ = Spider Web Rose

⌐ = Stem Stitch

— = Straight Stitch

- - - - = Whipped Running Stitch

Couching

This technique requires two ribbons, one to be flat on the fabric (usually wide) and the other (usually narrow) to hold the first one in place. Bring needle and wide ribbon up at 1, the left side of area to be covered. Pull ribbon through to the right and park it temporarily at side of fabric. Use your non-stitching thumb to hold wide ribbon flat as you "couch" it with the other ribbon (or floss).

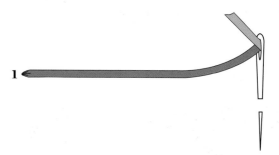

Bring second needle with narrow ribbon up at A, beneath wider ribbon at bottom of first couching point. Pass needle vertically over wider ribbon, and stitch down at top of first couching point, (B). Proceed to next couching point.

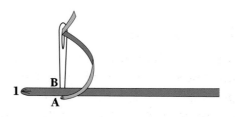

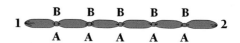

At end of row, pass wider ribbon needle through to back of fabric at 2 and secure it; hold couched ribbon flat with your thumb to prevent it from folding in on itself.

French Knot

When embroidering with ribbon, the French Knot is worked more loosely than when using floss or yarn. Bring needle up at 1 and wrap ribbon once or twice around shaft of needle. Swing point of needle clockwise and insert into fabric at 2, close to 1. Keep the working ribbon wrapped loosely around needle as you pull needle through to back of fabric. Release wrapping ribbon as knot is formed; do not pull the knot too tightly. You can change the size of the French Knot by using different ribbon widths, wrapping the ribbon one or more times around the needle, and/or varying your tension.

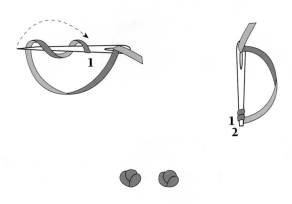

Loop Stitch

Bring needle up at 1, stitch down at 2 (close to 1), and pull ribbon part way through fabric. Insert a holding device (drinking straw, pencil, large tapestry needle, pin, etc.) through loop; pull ribbon snug to hold shape. Keep straw in place until the next petal is made in the same manner, then remove straw. If desired, these upright petals can be tacked in place.

Padded Straight Stitch

Make a Straight Stitch (1-2), page 9, then work a longer Straight Stitch directly over the first one, (3-4), to create volume.

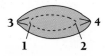

Lazy Daisy Stitch

Bring needle up at 1 and flatten the ribbon as it emerges from fabric. Re-insert needle next to 1 (skipping a thread or two to avoid piercing ribbon), and pull until the loop is desired length. Bring needle up at 3 at the bottom of the stitch. Pull the ribbon through until desired shape is formed. Re-insert needle over the loop at 4 (close to 3) to anchor it.

continued

Pistil Stitch

Bring needle up at 1 and wrap ribbon twice around shaft of needle. Swing point of needle clockwise and insert into fabric at 2, the indicated distance from 1. Pull working ribbon around needle; hold wrap with thumb and forefinger of your non-stitching hand, as you pull needle and ribbon through to back of fabric.

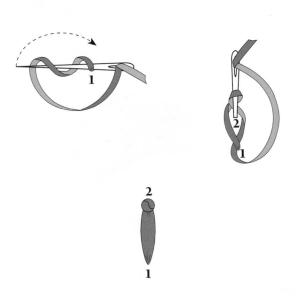

Ribbon Stitch

Bring needle up at 1 and flatten ribbon as it emerges through fabric. Extend ribbon just beyond length of intended stitch and insert needle through top surface of ribbon at 2. Pull ribbon gently through fabric as the sides of ribbon curl inward to form a point. Leave curls showing by not pulling too tightly. Vary this stitch by using different ribbon widths and tension.

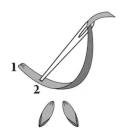

Side Ribbon Stitch

Begin as if for a Ribbon Stitch (previous stitch), but insert needle close to one edge of ribbon. Continue to pull gently until desired shape for tip is achieved.

Spider Web Rose

Make a weaving base of five evenly spaced legs radiating from center. Bring needle up at 1 and down at 2, creating a "V." Bring needle up at 3, above point of V, then stitch down at 4. Add two more legs (5-6 and 7-8) to create the base. End off ribbon.

Bring a different ribbon up at center of web and begin weaving over and under the five legs in a circular manner until the desired fullness is achieved. To end, insert needle beneath rose and pull gently through fabric. Do not worry about twists—they add interest and dimension.

8

Stem Stitch

Bring needle up at 1. Use the thumb of your non-stitching hand to hold ribbon flat. Insert needle at 2 and come up at 3, then pull ribbon through. Continue in this manner, with ribbon held below your stitching.

Whipped Running Stitch

Begin by working Running Stitches: Bring ribbon up at 1 and stitch down at 2; continue to desired length of line. Bring ribbon back up at A, close to end of last stitch. Wrap by slipping needle once or twice under the stitch. Continue in this manner and stitch down to end.

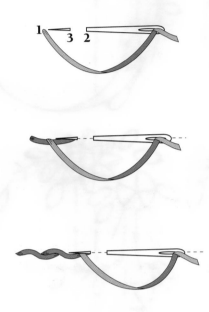

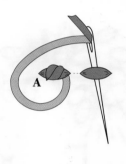

Straight Stitch

Bring needle from back of fabric at beginning point of stitch (1). Flatten ribbon with non-stitching thumb beyond intended length of stitch, and stitch down at opposite end of stitch (2). Pull gently, keeping the stitch flat.

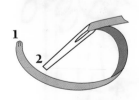

Cover Guide

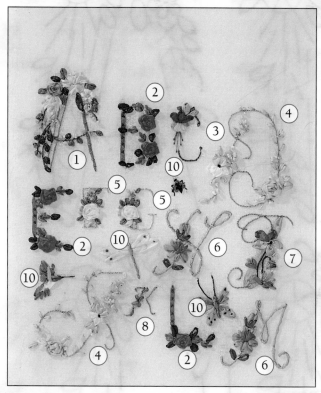

Front Cover

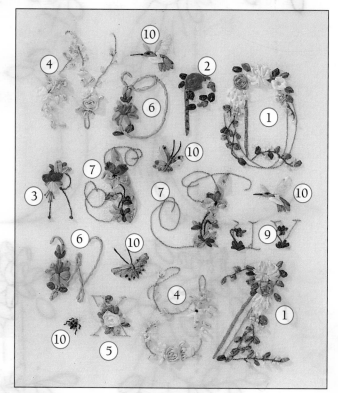

Back Cover

The numbers on each guide refer to the alphabet listing below. For each alphabet, page numbers are given for both the Transfers and the Stitching Guide.

Alphabet Guide	Transfers	Stitching Guides
1. Garden Delight	11-15	48
2. Really Red Roses	17-19	49
3. Fluttering Fuchsias	21	49
4. Spring Bouquet	23-29	50
5. Pretty Pastels	31	51
6. Floral Fantasy	33-35	51
7. Purple Pansies	37-43	52
8. Peeking Pinks	43	52
9. Nodding Violets	45	53
10. Garden Creatures	45	53-56

Test Pattern

Test Pattern

Test Pattern

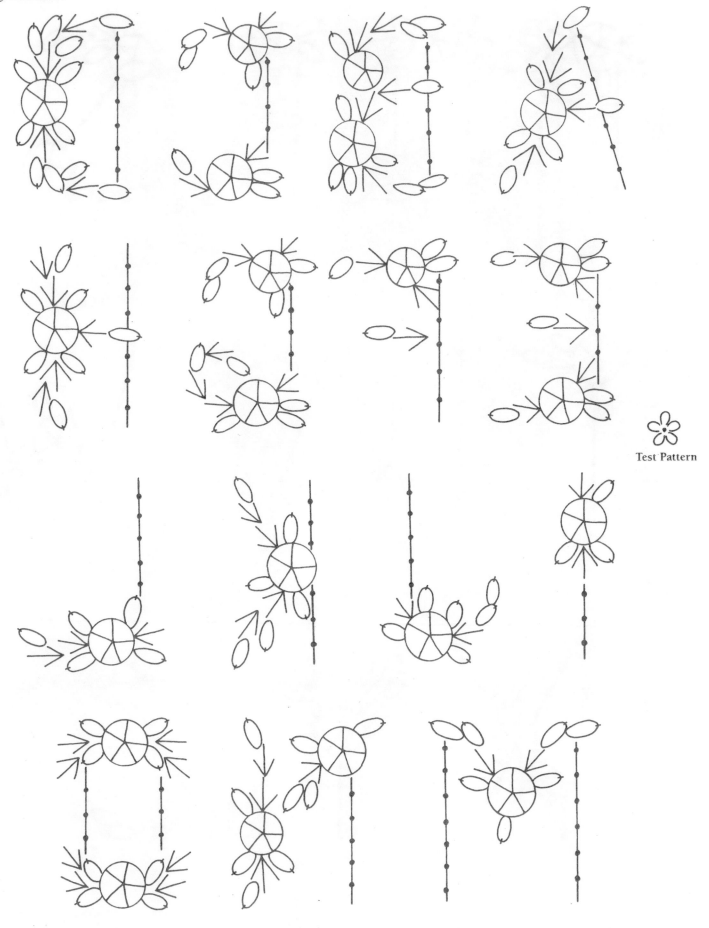

Test Pattern

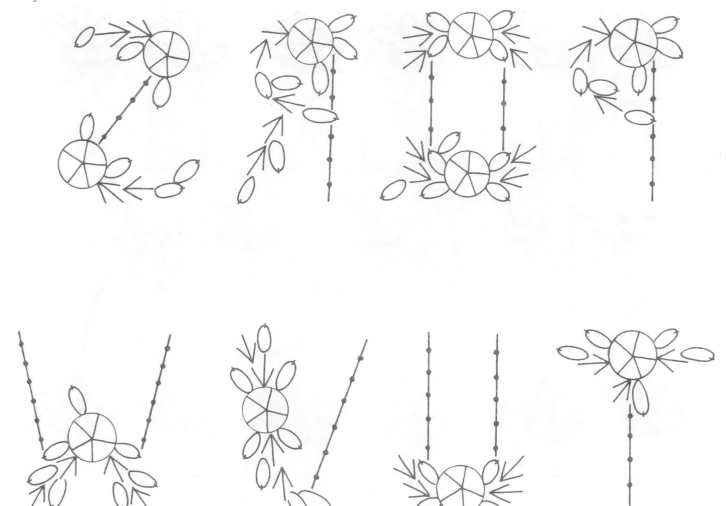

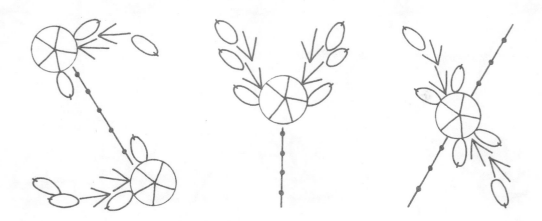

Test Pattern

Test Pattern

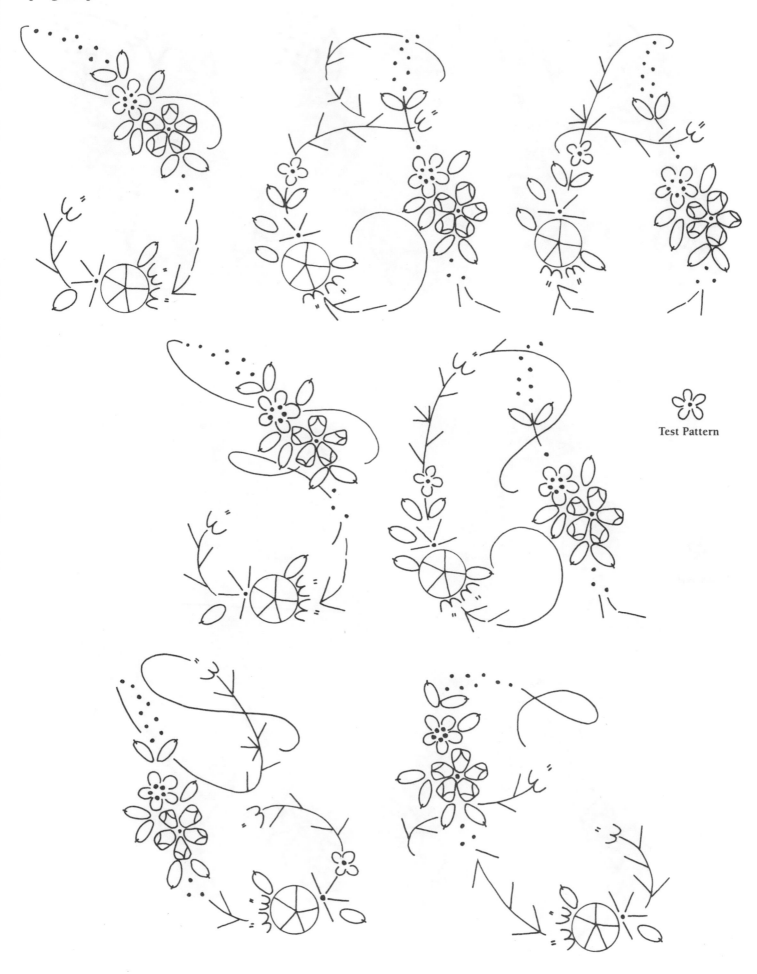

Test Pattern

Spring Bouquet

Test Pattern

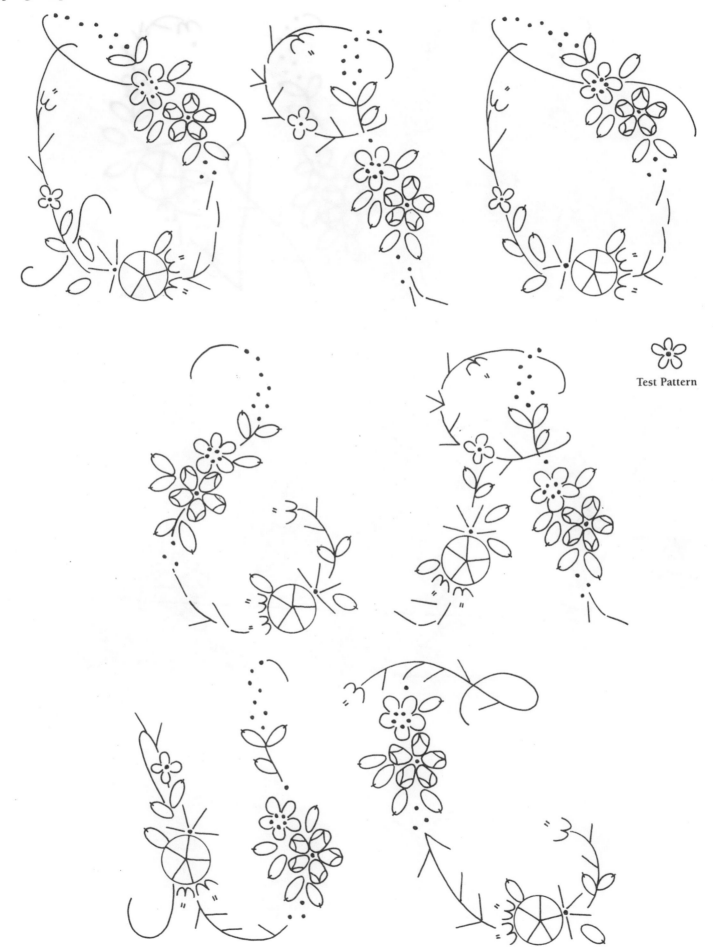

Test Pattern

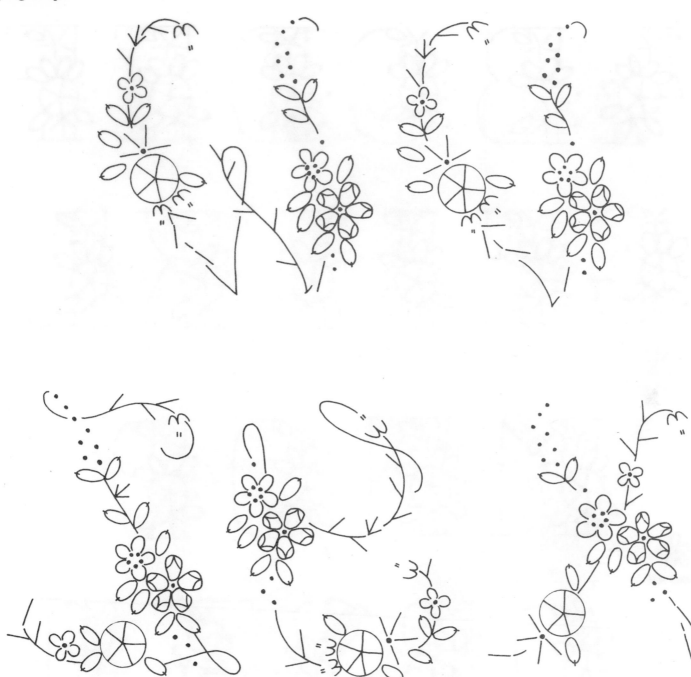

Test Pattern

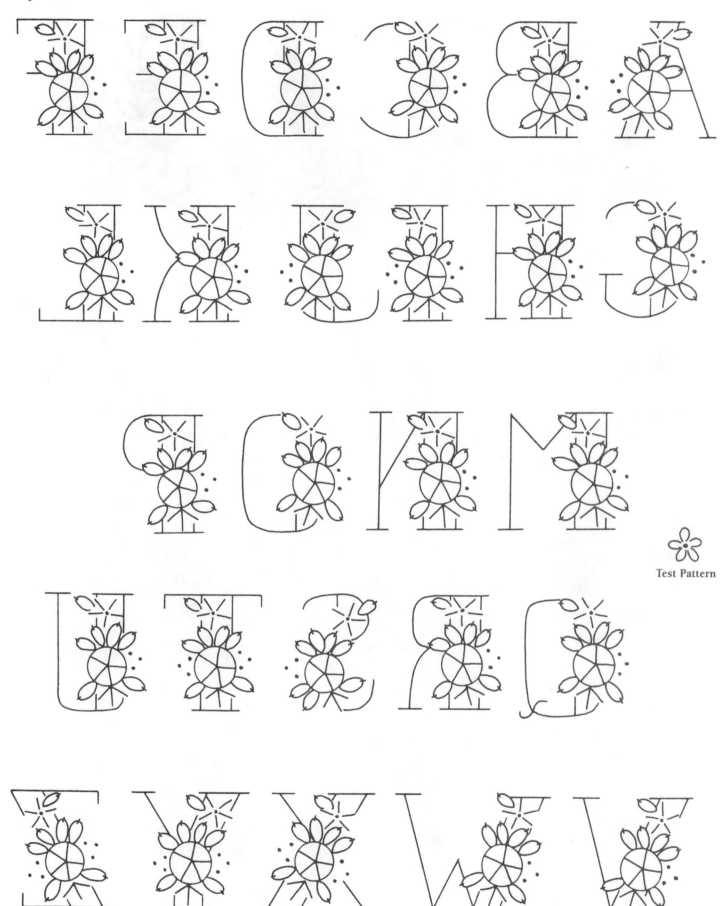

Test Pattern

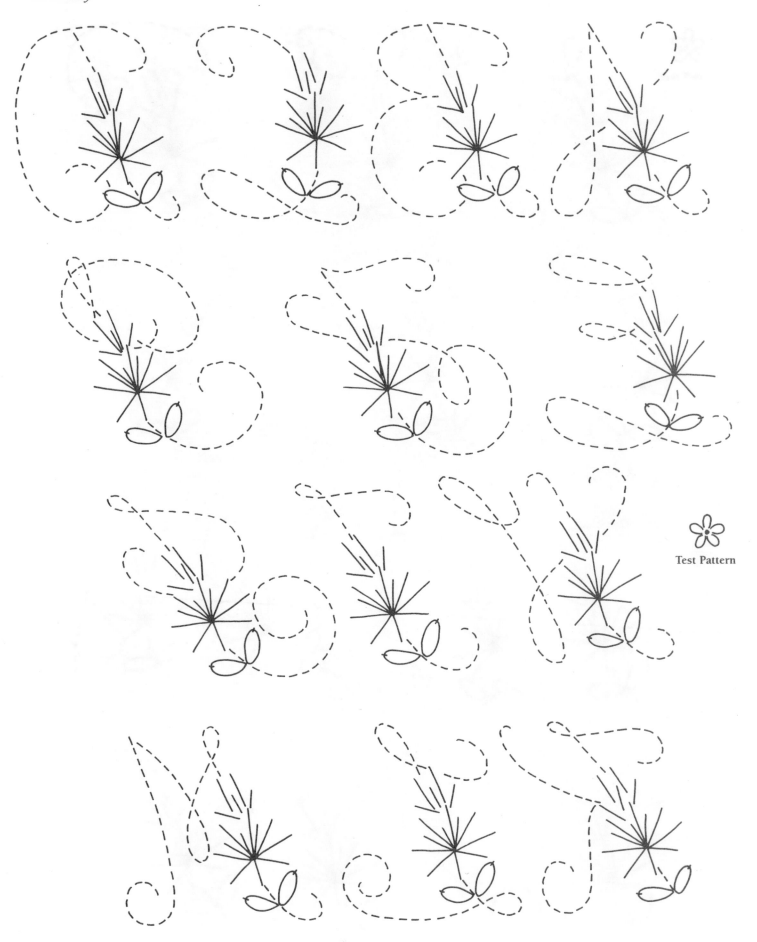

Test Pattern

Test Pattern

Test Pattern

Test Pattern

Test Pattern

Purple Pansies & Peeking Pinks

Test Pattern

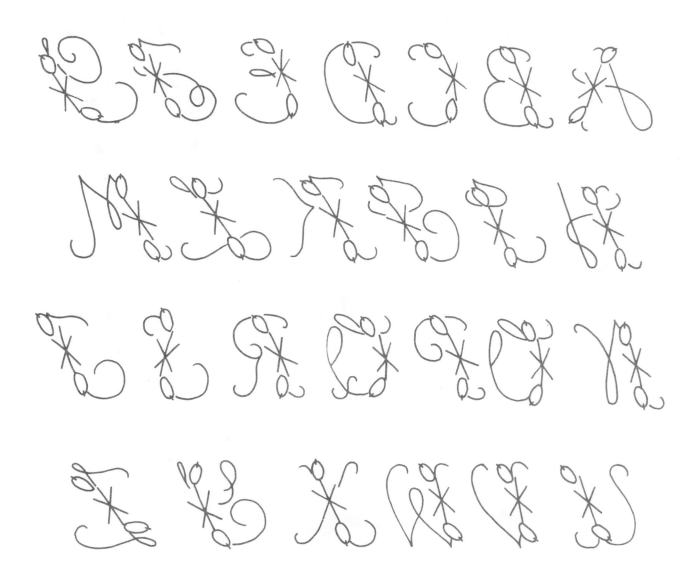

43

Test Pattern

Alphabet Stitching Guides

We chose one letter (shown on the front or the back cover) from each alphabet and have a Stitching Guide for that letter. The Stitching Guide lists the ribbon color and size plus the stitches required for each letter. Use the information to stitch any of the letters in the same alphabet.

The designs use symbols to show the shape of each stitch in addition to the placement. Following is a list of the symbols and the stitches they represent.

SYMBOLS FOR STITCHES

┼┼┼	= Couching
•	= French Knot
𝒪	= Lazy Daisy Stitch
𝒪	= Loop Stitch
"	= Padded Straight Stitch
'	= Pistil Stitch
𝒪	= Ribbon Stitch
𝒪	= Side Ribbon Stitch
⊕	= Spider Web Rose
∿	= Stem Stitch
—	= Straight Stitch
– – – –	= Whipped Running Stitch

Garden Delight

Note: *Refer to cover photograph for suggested placement of dark yellow-green or dark green leaves.*

Stitching order

Use medium green floss to Stem-Stitch part of the letter outline. Position medium yellow-green 2mm ribbon on fabric; if desired, pin in place. Couch with medium green floss to complete letter outline. Remove pins. Work remaining Stem Stitches in dark green floss.

Flowers—On Side Ribbon Stitch flower, work outer stitches first, then finish toward center. To make ivory and peach flower cascade: Work ivory Straight Stitches first; place a shorter medium yellow Straight Stitch on top, then a very short dark peach Straight Stitch at tip of ivory stitch. Work remaining flowers.

Buds—Straight-Stitch the buds, then work the leaves.

Leaves—Work dark yellow-green and dark green Lazy Daisy Stitches in desired arrangement.

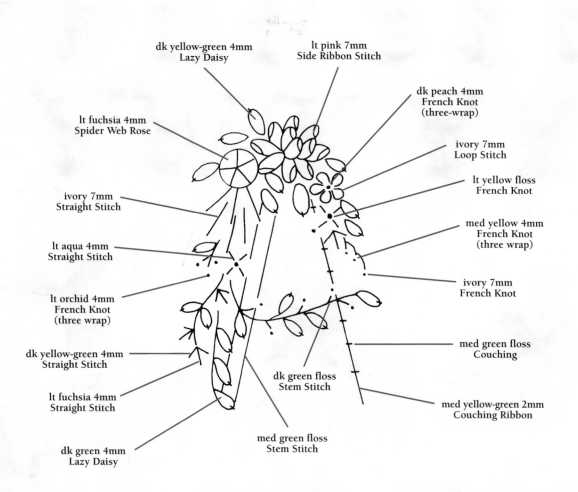

dk yellow-green 4mm
Lazy Daisy

lt pink 7mm
Side Ribbon Stitch

dk peach 4mm
French Knot
(three-wrap)

lt fuchsia 4mm
Spider Web Rose

ivory 7mm
Loop Stitch

lt yellow floss
French Knot

ivory 7mm
Straight Stitch

med yellow 4mm
French Knot
(three wrap)

lt aqua 4mm
Straight Stitch

ivory 7mm
French Knot

lt orchid 4mm
French Knot
(three wrap)

med green floss
Couching

dk yellow-green 4mm
Straight Stitch

dk green floss
Stem Stitch

med yellow-green 2mm
Couching Ribbon

lt fuchsia 4mm
Straight Stitch

dk green 4mm
Lazy Daisy

med green floss
Stem Stitch

Really Red Roses

Stitching order

Make a Straight Stitch with medium yellow-green 4mm ribbon on fabric; if desired, pin in place. Use dark green floss to work French Knots on top of ribbon. Remove pins.

Buds—Where three Straight Stitches share a common base, work the center stitch first in bud color, then work a leaf on each side of bud. Work Spider Web Rose last.

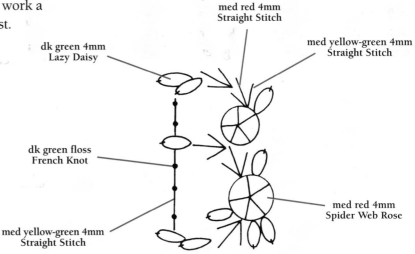

dk green 4mm
Lazy Daisy

med red 4mm
Straight Stitch

med yellow-green 4mm
Straight Stitch

dk green floss
French Knot

med red 4mm
Spider Web Rose

med yellow-green 4mm
Straight Stitch

Fluttering Fuchsias

Stitching order

Use green floss to Stem-Stitch letter outline.

Flower—For bottom half, work dark pink Straight Stitches at edges, then medium pink and light pink toward center. For top half, work dark red Ribbon Stitches, overlapping previous stitches.

Leaves—Work medium light green Straight Stitches, then light green Lazy Daisy Stitches. Use dark red floss for Pistil Stitches.

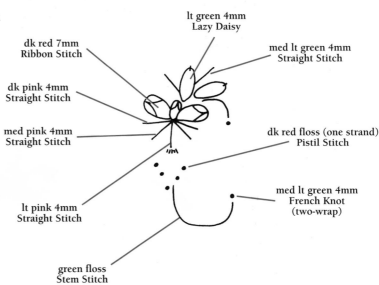

lt green 4mm
Lazy Daisy

dk red 7mm
Ribbon Stitch

med lt green 4mm
Straight Stitch

dk pink 4mm
Straight Stitch

med pink 4mm
Straight Stitch

dk red floss (one strand)
Pistil Stitch

med lt green 4mm
French Knot
(two-wrap)

lt pink 4mm
Straight Stitch

green floss
Stem Stitch

Spring Bouquet

Note: *When three Straight Stitches radiate from the stem, work the middle stitch in light blue-gray and the outer stitches in light gray-green to form a bud.*

Stitching order

Use medium green floss to Stem-Stitch letter outline. Work leaves and individual French Knots (in desired colors) first. Work Padded Straight Stitch buds, then medium green floss Straight Stitches. Make Ribbon Stitch flowers, extending petal length beyond transfer line. Make Straight Stitch flowers next, then Loop Stitch flowers, and work Spider Web Rose last.

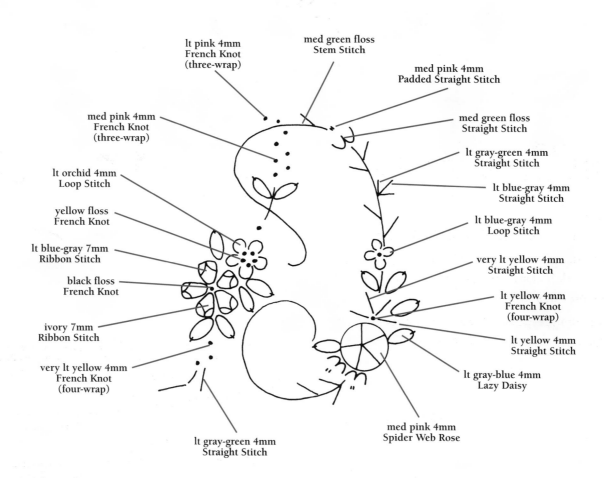

lt pink 4mm
French Knot
(three-wrap)

med green floss
Stem Stitch

med pink 4mm
Padded Straight Stitch

med pink 4mm
French Knot
(three-wrap)

med green floss
Straight Stitch

lt gray-green 4mm
Straight Stitch

lt blue-gray 4mm
Straight Stitch

lt orchid 4mm
Loop Stitch

lt blue-gray 4mm
Loop Stitch

yellow floss
French Knot

very lt yellow 4mm
Straight Stitch

lt blue-gray 7mm
Ribbon Stitch

black floss
French Knot

lt yellow 4mm
French Knot
(four-wrap)

ivory 7mm
Ribbon Stitch

lt yellow 4mm
Straight Stitch

very lt yellow 4mm
French Knot
(four-wrap)

lt gray-blue 4mm
Lazy Daisy

med pink 4mm
Spider Web Rose

lt gray-green 4mm
Straight Stitch

Pretty Pastels

Stitching order

Use turquoise floss to Stem-Stitch letter outline. Work remaining flowers and leaves with ribbon, making Spider Web Rose last.

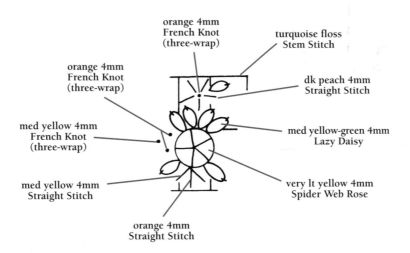

orange 4mm French Knot (three-wrap)

turquoise floss Stem Stitch

orange 4mm French Knot (three-wrap)

dk peach 4mm Straight Stitch

med yellow 4mm French Knot (three-wrap)

med yellow-green 4mm Lazy Daisy

med yellow 4mm Straight Stitch

very lt yellow 4mm Spider Web Rose

orange 4mm Straight Stitch

Floral Fantasy

Stitching order

Work Whipped Running Stitch letter outline first.

Flower—Work light fuchsia Straight Stitches, then work two or three dark fuchsia Straight Stitches at center, overlapping previous stitches.

Bud—Work Straight Stitches for bud first, then overlapping Straight Stitch leaves. Work Lazy Daisy leaves last.

lt green 4mm Whipped Running Stitch

lt fuchsia 4mm Straight Stitch

lt fuchsia 7mm Straight Stitch

med lt green 4mm Straight Stitch

dk fuchsia 7mm Straight Stitch

med lt green 4mm Lazy Daisy

Purple Pansies

Stitching order

Make a Straight Stitch with mauve 7mm ribbon on fabric; if desired, pin in place. Use mauve floss to work French Knots on top of ribbon. Remove pins. Stem-Stitch letter outline with mauve floss and flower stems with dark green floss.

Flower—Work dark orchid and dark blue-gray Ribbon Stitches. Work dark yellow Straight Stitches, then work black floss Straight Stitches on top, and end with black floss French Knot.

Buds—Work bud first, then leaves.

Leaves—Work dark gray-green, then medium yellow-green Straight Stitches.

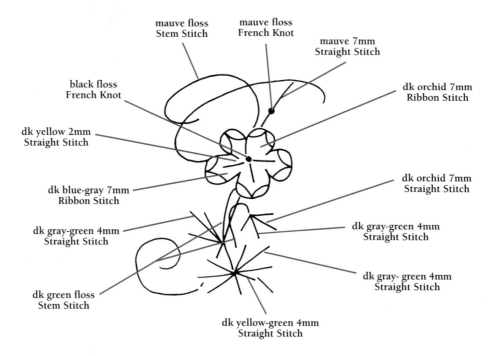

- mauve floss Stem Stitch
- mauve floss French Knot
- mauve 7mm Straight Stitch
- black floss French Knot
- dk orchid 7mm Ribbon Stitch
- dk yellow 2mm Straight Stitch
- dk orchid 7mm Straight Stitch
- dk blue-gray 7mm Ribbon Stitch
- dk gray-green 4mm Straight Stitch
- dk gray-green 4mm Straight Stitch
- dk gray-green 4mm Straight Stitch
- dk green floss Stem Stitch
- dk yellow-green 4mm Straight Stitch

Peeking Pinks

Stitching order

Use medium green floss to Stem-Stitch letter outline. Straight-Stitch the pink flower buds. Straight-Stitch overlapping leaves on each side of the buds; then work Lazy Daisy leaves.

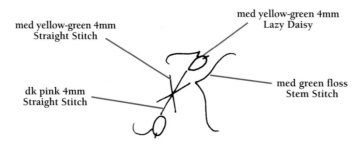

- med yellow-green 4mm Straight Stitch
- med yellow-green 4mm Lazy Daisy
- dk pink 4mm Straight Stitch
- med green floss Stem Stitch

Nodding Violets

Stitching order

Use turquoise floss to Stem-Stitch letter outline. Use medium green floss to Stem-Stitch stem. At tip of flower stem, work two overlapping Straight Stitches at center for violet blossom and three overlapping Straight Stitches for the calyx. Work overlapping Straight Stitches at base of flower stem.

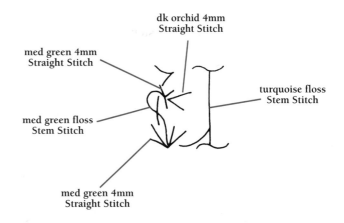

dk orchid 4mm
Straight Stitch

med green 4mm
Straight Stitch

turquoise floss
Stem Stitch

med green floss
Stem Stitch

med green 4mm
Straight Stitch

Butterflies

Stitching order

Blue Butterfly—Work Whipped Running Stitch body first. Beginning at top of body on each side, work one dark aqua, two light blue, then two or three dark aqua Straight Stitches for wings. Use medium red ribbon to work medium Straight Stitches on upper wings and short Straight Stitches over ends of lower wings. Use floss to work antennae and French Knots last.

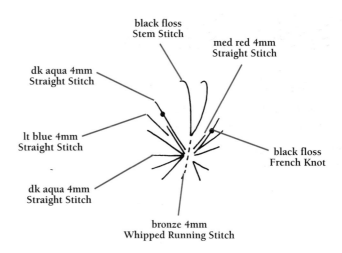

black floss
Stem Stitch

med red 4mm
Straight Stitch

dk aqua 4mm
Straight Stitch

lt blue 4mm
Straight Stitch

black floss
French Knot

dk aqua 4mm
Straight Stitch

bronze 4mm
Whipped Running Stitch

continued

Butterflies (continued)

Stitching order

Turquoise Butterfly—Work Whipped Running Stitch body first. Work turquoise Straight Stitches for lower wings, then dark blue Straight Stitches for upper wings. Work short dark blue Straight Stitches on top of lower wings and purple Straight Stitches on top of upper wings. Use floss to work antennae and French Knots.

black floss
Stem Stitch

purple 4mm
Straight Stitch

dk blue 4mm
Straight Stitch

black floss
French Knot

bronze 4mm
Whipped Running Stitch

turquoise 4mm
Straight Stitch

Stitching order

Rose Butterfly—Work Whipped Running Stitch body first. Work Straight Stitches for the wings: light fuchsia under medium fuchsia for upper wings, medium rose for bottom wings, then light and medium rose for middle wings. Use floss to work antennae and French Knots.

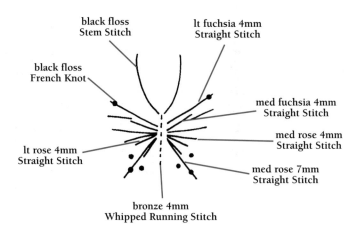

black floss
Stem Stitch

lt fuchsia 4mm
Straight Stitch

black floss
French Knot

med fuchsia 4mm
Straight Stitch

med rose 4mm
Straight Stitch

lt rose 4mm
Straight Stitch

med rose 7mm
Straight Stitch

bronze 4mm
Whipped Running Stitch

Hummingbirds

Stitching order

Blue Hummingbird—Work body, head, tail, then back feathers (including cap on head), all with Straight Stitches. Work light yellow, then dark yellow Straight Stitches for wings, with bottom light yellow stitch covering shoulder joint. Use floss for eye and beak.

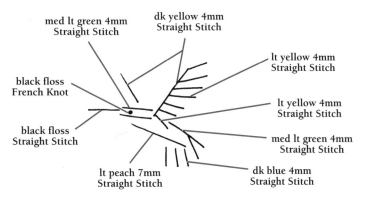

med lt green 4mm Straight Stitch

dk yellow 4mm Straight Stitch

lt yellow 4mm Straight Stitch

black floss French Knot

lt yellow 4mm Straight Stitch

black floss Straight Stitch

med lt green 4mm Straight Stitch

lt peach 7mm Straight Stitch

dk blue 4mm Straight Stitch

Stitching order

Brown Hummingbird—Work body, head, tail, then back feathers (including cap on head), all with Straight Stitches. Work wing and tail feathers. Work light yellow wing feather to cover shoulder joint. Use floss for eye and beak.

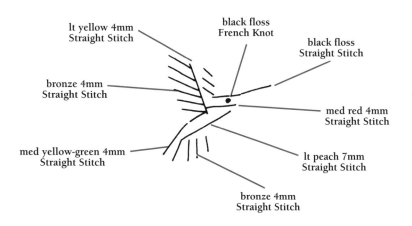

lt yellow 4mm Straight Stitch

black floss French Knot

black floss Straight Stitch

bronze 4mm Straight Stitch

med red 4mm Straight Stitch

med yellow-green 4mm Straight Stitch

lt peach 7mm Straight Stitch

bronze 4mm Straight Stitch

Dragonfly

Stitching order

Work turquoise Whipped Running Stitch body first.
For wings, work long medium peach Straight Stitches,
then, using a more narrow ribbon, work shorter very
light yellow Straight Stitches on top. Use floss to work
French Knots last.

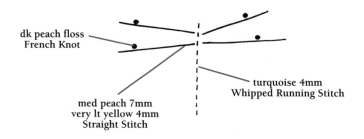

dk peach floss
French Knot

turquoise 4mm
Whipped Running Stitch

med peach 7mm
very lt yellow 4mm
Straight Stitch

Ladybug

Stitching order

Straight-Stitch black body and head. Work medium red
Straight Stitches for wings overlapping previous stitches.
Use floss to work French Knots and Straight Stitch
legs last.

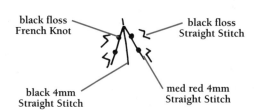

black floss
French Knot

black floss
Straight Stitch

black 4mm
Straight Stitch

med red 4mm
Straight Stitch